RENDILLE

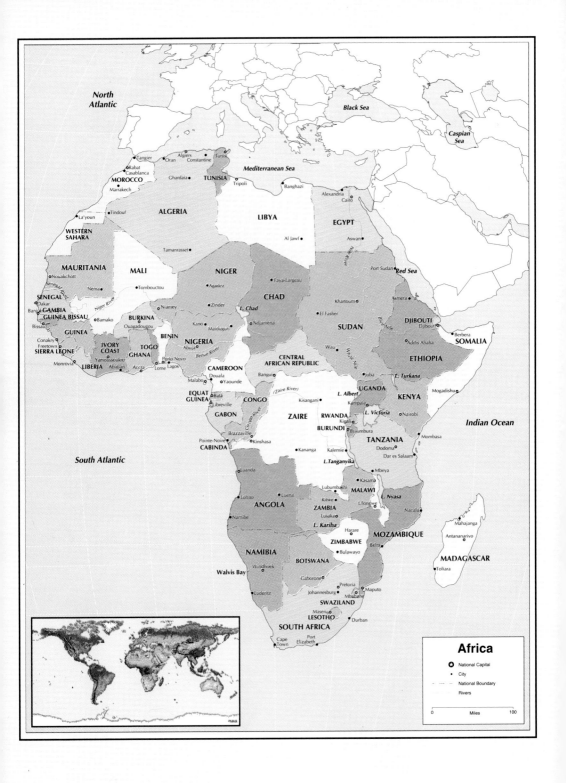

North
Atlantic

Black Sea

Caspian
Sea

Tangier
Algiers Tunis
Rabat Oran Constantine
Casablanca
MOROCCO Ghardaia
Marrakech
TUNISIA
Mediterranean Sea
Tripoli
Banghazi
Alexandria
Cairo

La'youn Tindouf
ALGERIA
LIBYA
EGYPT
WESTERN
SAHARA
Al Jawf
Aswan

MAURITANIA
Nouakchott
Nema
MALI
Tombouctou
Tamanrasset

NIGER
Agadez
Faya-Largeau

Port Sudan
Red Sea

Asmera

SENEGAL
Dakar
GAMBIA
Banjul
GUINEA BISSAU
Bissau
GUINEA
Conakry
Freetown
SIERRA LEONE
Monrovia
LIBERIA
Senegal River
Niger River
Niamey
Bamako
BURKINA
Ouagadougou
BENIN
NIGERIA
Abuja
IVORY
COAST
Yamoussoukro
GHANA
Abidjan
Accra
TOGO
Porto Novo
Lome Lagos
Zinder
Kano
Maiduguri
CHAD
L. Chad
Ndjamena
Benue River
CAMEROON
Douala
Yaounde
CENTRAL
AFRICAN REPUBLIC
Bangui
Khartoum
El Fasher
SUDAN
Wau
White Nile
Blue Nile
DJIBOUTI
Djibouti
Berbera
Addis Ababa
SOMALIA
ETHIOPIA
Juba
L. Turkana
Mogadishu

EQUAT.
GUINEA
Malabo
Bata
Libreville
CONGO
GABON
Brazzaville
Pointe-Noire
CABINDA
Kinshasa
ZAIRE
(Zaire River)
Kisangani
Congo River
RWANDA
Kigali
BURUNDI
Bujumbura
L. Albert
Kampala
L. Victoria
UGANDA
KENYA
Nairobi
Mombasa
Kananga
Kalemie
TANZANIA
Dodoma
Dar es Salaam
L. Tanganyika

Indian Ocean

South Atlantic

Luanda
Lobito
Namibe
ANGOLA
Luena
Lubumbashi
Kitwe
ZAMBIA
Lusaka
L. Kariba
Kasama
Mbeya
MALAWI
Lilongwe
L. Nyasa
Nacala

Walvis Bay
NAMIBIA
Windhoek
Luderitz
BOTSWANA
Gaborone
Harare
ZIMBABWE
Bulawayo
Beira
MOZAMBIQUE

Mahajanga
Antananarivo
MADAGASCAR
Toliara

Pretoria
Johannesburg
Maputo
Mbabane
SWAZILAND
Maseru
LESOTHO
SOUTH AFRICA
Cape
Town
Port
Elizabeth
Durban

Africa

⊗ National Capital
• City
--- National Boundary
Rivers

0   Miles   100

RENDILLE

Ronald G. Parris, Ph.D.

THE ROSEN PUBLISHING GROUP, INC.
NEW YORK

To Kira Danielle, in the hope that she will grow up even more fully aware of our African heritage.

Published in 1994 by The Rosen Publishing Group, Inc.
29 East 21st Street, New York, NY 10010

First Edition

Manufactured in the United States of America

Library of Congress Cataloging-in-Publication Data

Parris, Ronald G.
    Rendille / Ronald G. Parris. — 1st ed.
      p. cm. — (The Heritage library of African Peoples)
    Includes bibliographical references (p.   ) and index.
    ISBN 0-8239-1763-0
    1. Rendile (African People) — Juvenile literature. [1. Rendile
(African people)] I. Title. II. Series.
    DT433.545.R45P37   1994
    967.62′4—dc20   94-7246
                                                  CIP
                                                     AC

Contents

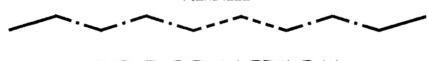

INTRODUCTION

THERE IS EVERY REASON FOR US TO KNOW something about Africa and to understand its past and the way of life of its peoples. Africa is a rich continent that has for centuries provided the world with art, culture, labor, wealth, and natural resources. It has vast mineral deposits, fossil fuels, and commercial crops.

But perhaps most important is the fact that fossil evidence indicates that human beings originated in Africa. The earliest traces of human beings and their tools are almost two million years old. Their descendants have migrated throughout the world. To be human is to be of African descent.

The experiences of the peoples who stayed in Africa are as rich and as diverse as of those who established themselves elsewhere. This series of books describes their environment, their modes of subsistence, their relationships, and their customs and beliefs. They present the variety of languages, histories, cultures, and religions that are to be found on the African continent. The books demonstrate the historical linkages between African peoples and the way contemporary Africa has been affected by European colonial rule.

Africa is large, complex, and diverse. It encompasses an area of more than 11,700,000 square miles. The United States, Europe, and India could fit easily into it. The sheer size is an indication of the continent's great variety in geography, terrain, climate, flora, fauna, peoples, languages, and cultures.

Much of contemporary Africa has been shaped by European colonial rule, industrialization, urbanization, and the demands of a world economic system. For more than seventy years, large regions of Africa were ruled by Great Britain, France, Belgium, Portugal, and Spain. African peoples from various ethnic, linguistic, and cultural backgrounds were brought together to form colonial states.

For decades Africans struggled to gain their independence. It was not until after World War II that the colonial territories became independent African states. Today, almost all of Africa is ruled by Africans. Large numbers of Africans live in modern cities. Rural Africa is also being transformed, and yet its people still engage in many of their age-old customs and beliefs.

Contemporary circumstances and natural events have not always been kind to ordinary Africans. Today, however, new popular social movements and technological innovations pose great promise for future development.

George C. Bond
Institute of African Studies
Columbia University, New York City

The Rendille have learned to survive the harsh conditions of the Kaisut Desert.

chapter

1

THE LAND AND THE PEOPLE

THE RENDILLE ARE A RELATIVELY SMALL group known throughout Africa for their ability to adapt to and survive the harsh conditions of the Kaisut Desert in central Kenya.

The Rendille are a graceful people who like to decorate their bodies with beads and ornaments. They are nomadic herders who settle in one place for a while and then move on at the change of the season to find new grazing land for their camels. The Marsabit District of north central Kenya is their home: They live in the scrub of the Korante Plains and the rocks of the Kaisut Desert, southeast of Lake Turkana. The Marsabit Mountains lie to the northeast, linking Kenya with Ethiopia. The Chalbi Desert is the northern border, and the Ndoto Mountains are to the south.

The north and east parts of this land are low,

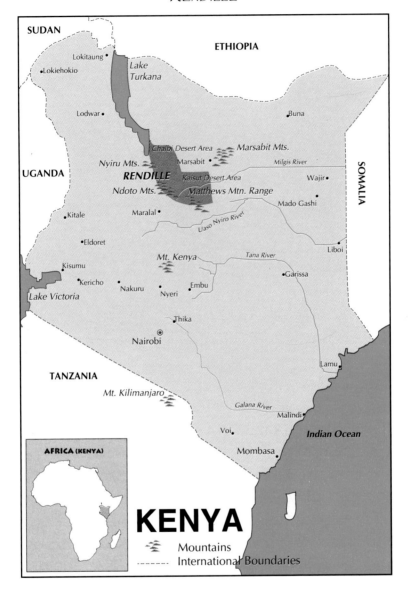

SUDAN

ETHIOPIA

Lokitaung •
Lake
Turkana
•Lokiehokio

Lodwar •

Buna•

Chalbi Desert Area   Marsabit Mts.
Nyiru Mts.   Marsabit •   Milgis River

UGANDA   **RENDILLE**   Kaisut Desert Area   Wajir•
Ndoto Mts.   Matthews Mtn. Range   Mado Gashi•

•Kitale   Maralal •   Uaso Nyiro River

•Eldoret   Liboi•

Kisumu   Mt. Kenya   Tana River

•Kericho   Nakuru   Embu   •Garissa
Lake Victoria   Nyeri

Thika

Nairobi

Lamu•

TANZANIA

Mt. Kilimanjaro
Galana River
Malindi•
Voi•   **Indian Ocean**
Mombasa•

AFRICA (KENYA)

KENYA

🌿 Mountains
------- International Boundaries

SOMALIA

dry, and hot. Vegetation is poor, and soil erosion
is extensive. Yet, in this land, the Rendille herd
their camels as well as sheep, goats, and some
cattle.

To the southwest, the land rises gradually.
The climate is less dry, and the land is more

suitable for cattle-herding. The neighboring
Samburu herd cattle in the area. Continuing
southwest along Mount Ngiro, the Ndoto
Mountains, and Matthews Range, the land rises.
The climate is cooler in these grasslands. The
Ariaal, a major subgroup of the Rendille, herd
their cattle here. This area is now considered the
territory of the Samburu. Rendille land is in the
northeast, and their main livestock in that drier
area is camels, not cattle.

The Rendille depend on rainfall as the main
source of water. The Marsabit District receives
about 30 inches of rainfall a year. The Kaisut
Desert, the driest region in Kenya, gets only half
that much.

There are two major rainy seasons: March to
May, and October and November. The remain-
ing months are drought-stricken.

One must consider the climatic conditions
that affect the Rendille and Samburu in order to
understand the Rendille. The rainfall patterns on
the western side of the mountains, where the
Samburu live, is heavy in contrast to the low,
arid land of the Rendille. In the dry regions,
water remains visible only for a few days on the
main waterways, Lake Rudolph and Uaso Ngiro
River. It quickly seeps several feet below the
surface. The only way to get at it is to dig water
holes. Whoever uses a water hole is considered
its owner.

RAIN FESTIVALS

The Rendille mark the end of a rainy season with a ceremony of thanks for the rains, because they will keep the grass growing and the wells full of water for a while. Such ceremonies are held in January and February and in June and July. The Rendille living in the camel camps come back to the settlements for these observances.

The coming of heavy rains in April is also celebrated with prayers for rain and the good fortune of the settlement. This is a ceremony for the elders and their wives, not the youths of the camel camps. It is a long and elaborate ceremony performed by various age-sets. Just outside the enclosure that is built for the *Nabo* (*Naapo*) ceremony, where the age-sets are initiated into elderhood, the men drink milk and smoke tobacco. After seven days, the elders shave their heads and drink a herbal brew prepared by their wives. All say a blessing together. With the wives leading, a procession is held as horns play and ritual fires burn on either side. The wives are followed by a procession of small stock, with the elders bringing up the rear.

The Rendille are one of the smallest ethnic groups in Kenya, with a population somewhere between 14,000 and 22,000. It is difficult to take a census of a nomadic people.

▼ WHO ARE THE RENDILLE? ▼
Two major subgroups make up the Rendille. The Northern or "True" Rendille number be-

tween 10,000 and 16,000. The Southern Rendille, known also as the Ariaal, number about 6,000. They are a mixture of Rendille and Samburu. Another group, called the Odola Rendille, are sometimes identified north of the Northern Rendille, between them and the Gabbra.

The difference between cattle-herding (pastoral) and farming groups is very important. A people's life-style defines their relationship with their environment and their social organization and customs. Pastoralists mainly herd cattle and camels for a living. Agricultural groups usually keep a few cattle, goats, and sheep on their farms. Some groups depend equally on farming and herding.

The Ariaal are nomadic pastoralists. They herd camels, cattle, and small stock such as sheep and goats. Living between the Northern Rendille and the Samburu, they cooperate with both neighbors. The Rendille and Samburu have had close ties for many generations. They intermarry and exchange cultural ideas even though they live in separate areas, speak different languages, and have very different life-styles.

Marriage between the Rendille and Samburu is subject to differences in customs. Young Rendille men are allowed to marry only at certain times, but the Samburu are not limited. Thus Samburu men often choose Rendille wives

THE PEOPLES WHO CAME TO KENYA

The Rendille are members of the Cushitic language group, who came to Kenya from southern Ethiopia. The Cushitic peoples of that area are divided into Southern and Eastern Cushites. The Southern Cushites can be traced back to the Late Stone Age. Around 2000 BC (about 4,000 years ago), they started to move out of the Ethiopian highlands and into Kenya, taking with them their language and customs.

The Yaaku were the earliest group of Eastern Cushites to come to Kenya. The Yaaku (also called the Mokokodo) began to move south about 1,000 years ago. After the Yaaku, other Cushitic groups such as the Somali and the Galla (also called the Oromo) came from southern Ethiopia. When the Somali arrived from the north, the Bantu peoples were trying to expand from the southwest, but the Somali defeated them.

In the 16th century the Oromo pushed the Somali out of the area. It is thought that the Somali split into three smaller groups at that time. One of the groups moved north and inland. This group perhaps became the Rendille, the Gabbra, and the Sakuye peoples. The Rendille continued to speak the Somali Cushite language, while the other two peoples adopted the Oromo language. Today some clans of the Rendille say that they were originally Somali, and some use Somali brands on their camels.

Ethnographers are not sure, however, that this is the true origin of the Rendille. Some historians think that camels were brought to East Africa by Arabs about a thousand years ago. Others say that the Rendille were already herding camels in Kenya before the Arabs brought their animals.

KENYA

≋ Mountains
------- International Boundaries
—·—·— Provincial Boundaries

when the Rendille men are not allowed to marry. Both the Samburu and Rendille practice polygamy, which means that a man can marry more than one wife.

In Rendille families, the eldest son inherits all his father's land, leaving younger sons with no land at all. Such disinherited men sometimes migrate to the Ariaal and Samburu areas to seek

15

The land in which the Rendille live is often dry and barren.

A village typical of the Northern Rendille.

A hut characteristic of the southern Rendille.

a better future. The Northern Rendille consider the Ariaal as real Rendille, although they have mixed their language and culture with those of the Samburu. ▲

chapter

2

TRADITIONAL RENDILLE SOCIETY

RENDILLE SOCIETY IS DIVIDED INTO *MOIETIES* or equal parts. Each *moiety* is divided into clans, and the clans are further divided into subclans and lineage groups.

A Rendille is a member of his father's clan. A woman joins the clan of the man she marries. The members of a clan consider themselves family or kin, descended from a common ancestor. The typical size of a Rendille clan is one hundred or more people living in one or two settlements. Clan members work together to produce food, make decisions, and keep the community going. A Rendille's place in society depends on how powerful his clan is.

Each clan is divided into two to eleven subclans and as many as thirty lineage groups. The longer a family or lineage group has been established, the greater the power and respect it receives. The hut of the most senior family is placed in the northwestern corner of a settlement. The other families are placed by seniority in a clockwise direction. The elder of the most senior family has the duty of leading daily prayers and ceremonial feasts.

For the Rendille, the clan is all-important. The individual is under the authority of the elders of his clan. Customs and rituals for birth, marriage, and death are set by the lineage group.

Each clan has its own identity and characteristics. It has a special object or animal called a totem, which bestows power and protection from evil. Each clan also has its own brand for camels. Song is important in the society. The clan has songs for weddings, to pray for rain, in celebration of successful raids, and in praise of husbands, the clan, and the new moon. The Rendille say that song "soothes their life." They also dance. Sometimes dance competitions are held between two or more clans.

One group among the Rendille is not considered part of the clan system: the Tumal, or blacksmiths. Because they do not herd camels, they do not have equal status with other Rendille. They are not allowed to marry Rendille women of other groups. Their male initiation ceremony is separate. Because they are believed to be different, they are exempt from some

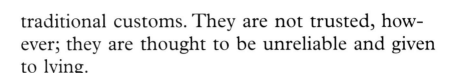

traditional customs. They are not trusted, however; they are thought to be unreliable and given to lying.

Behavior within and between clans is governed by strict rules that follow principles of honor, respect, and shame. There are even rules about who may tell a joke to whom.

The Ariaal clan system has some differences. Like the Northern Rendille, an Ariaal belongs to the clan of his father. However, the Ariaal also admit outsiders and relatives to make the clan larger. The Ariaal live in either cattle- or camel-herding settlements. Their subclans are connected to one of the Samburu *moieties*, and they use the clan names of the Samburu.

▼ AGE SYSTEM ▼

An important part of Rendille society is the system of age-grades and age-sets. Only males are assigned an age-set, but both sexes pass through age-grades. Age-grades are periods of life. Boyhood lasts from birth until circumcision, youth from circumcision to marriage, and elderhood from marriage until death. Elderhood is divided into junior, middle, senior, and retired elders.

To change age-grade from boyhood to youth, boys are circumcised and join an age-set. An age-set is made up of men who are about the

The Tumal, or blacksmiths, are not considered part of the clan system of the Rendille.

same age and who are initiated at the same time. Initiations of Rendille boys into age-sets occur every fourteen years.

Joining an age-set brings new responsibilities. The young men become herders and warriors, important to the survival and protection of their community. Each time an age-set is initiated, all the grades of elders move up to a more senior grade until reaching the final status of retired elders.

To move up in age-grade from youth to elder, the new age-set must wait about eleven years after the circumcision ceremony. At this

To move up in age-grade from youth to elder, the new age-set must wait about eleven years from the time of initiation.

time youths of different clans come together for the *Nabo* (*Naapo*) ceremony. This ritual shows that they are ready for elderhood and marriage. Before the next age-set is initiated

Elders are responsible for handling community problems.

three years later, those who have gone through
Nabo are expected to marry and become
elders.

Each age-set has a scapegoat, or *Dablakabire*.

23

Rendille girls have several responsibilities, including herding young animals and fetching water.

This person is believed to bring on the misfortunes of the whole age-set. The warrior chosen for *Dablakabire* usually accepts his fate.

Each age-grade has certain responsibilities. Boys begin taking care of young stock at age seven. At ten, they help with milking and herding of small livestock and camels. Youths are expected to manage and protect the livestock and in general to help look after the community.

Elders are responsible for handling community problems. Junior elders are expected to keep order. Middle elders are in charge of age-set ceremonies and help the senior elders with

AGE-SETS AND THE RENDILLE CALENDAR

The Rendille have a calendar of twelve months based on the cycles of the moon. The months are made up of weeks, each with seven days:

Gumad (Friday), *Sabdi* (Saturday), *Ahat* (Sunday), *Alasmin* (Monday), *Talaada* (Tuesday), *Arbah* (Wednesday), and *Khamis* (Thursday). Notice that Friday is the first day of the week.

Besides days, weeks, months, and years, the Rendille also think of time in seven-year blocks. In each block, the years have the same names as the days of the week. So the first year is always Gumad, the second is Sabdi, and so on.

This seven-year cycle is used to initiate new age-sets. Every fourteen years a new group of youths is initiated into an age-set. The ceremony always takes place in the year of Friday. A man is linked with other men in his age-set, and age-sets are linked to each other in groups of three. In other words, every fourteen years one age-set is initiated, and every forty-two years a link of three age-sets is initiated.

major decisions. Elders who have retired are greatly respected and are believed to have the power to bless and curse.

The age-grades for females are girlhood and womanhood. As with males, each age-grade has certain responsibilities. Girls join the boys in taking care of young animals in the settlement

The chart below shows links of age-sets, with their names and dates. Some of the names of age-sets can repeat, as long as they are in different links.

Age Set Links	Name of Age Set	Year of Initiation
I.	Irpaandif	1825
	Ilkubuku	1839
	Libali	1853
II.	Dibgudo	1867
	Dismala	1881
	Irbangudo	1895
III.	Difgudo	1909
	Irbales	1923
	Libale	1937
IV.	Irbandif	1951
	Difgudo	1965
	Irbangudo	1979

and livestock camp. After marriage, women give up herding. They build their hut in the settlement and take care of their children and household.▲

chapter

3

DAILY LIFE

THE FOUNDATION OF THE RENDILLE economic, social, and cultural life is camel-herding. Camel milk and blood are used as food. The camel carries the prefabricated house frame and household items that nomads move with them. It also transports water from wells to settlements.

Camels are the most valuable possession of the Rendille. All the camels in a family are owned by one man. Camel herds are difficult to build up and manage. Keeping the family herd together also gives the father greater control over his sons. They must add any camels of their own to the father's herd until they marry or the father dies. At the father's death, the eldest son of his first wife receives the whole herd and becomes head of the family. He gives a small number of stock to his younger brothers.

Camels are the most valuable possession of the Rendille.

The Rendille mostly herd camels rather than cattle because of the arid climate. Camels can travel as far as forty miles per day in this environment, whereas cows can manage only about ten. A pack camel can carry up to 200 pounds for six to eight hours. Camels can go without water for as long as ten days in dry weather, but cows must drink every three days. Also, camels give three or four times as much milk as cows.

Camel-herding is usually performed by young unmarried men of the warrior age-set. They must be able to travel as great distances as the camels do. They must trace and bring back

A camel can travel as far as forty miles a day in an arid climate.

animals that stray, a task that sometimes takes a week or more. The Rendille never ride their camels, except the sick or very old.

Another disadvantage of camel-herding is that it takes a long time for them to bear young. A camel bears its first calf at six years, whereas a cow can begin having calves at two and a half. Camel herds are also subject to serious and fatal diseases.

While the men tend the camels, women are busy fetching water and firewood, cooking, and caring for children. Before marriage, they help with herding the small livestock.

Rendille women make necklaces and brass

Rendille Foods

The staple food of the Rendille is camel milk. It is estimated that two healthy female camels can provide enough nourishment for a Rendille couple and several children. On ritual or ceremonial occasions, the meat of sheep and goats is eaten. Corn is sometimes eaten by pregnant women if milk is in short supply. In recent famines, corn has become an important food.

A typical day in the life of a Rendille might have an eating plan something like this:

7:00–7:30 am   Breakfast: Tea with milk, unboiled milk for the children.
10:00–10:30 am   Tea with milk, flavored with a local ginger called *gathaha*.
12:00–12:30 pm   Lunch: Porridge made of corn and flavored with sugar and salt. Sometimes sour milk is also used as a flavoring, tasting something like plain yogurt.
4:00–4:30 pm   Tea with milk.
7:00–7:30 pm   Dinner: Porridge, as at lunchtime.

Although the Rendille do sometimes eat meat, they prefer not to slaughter or hunt animals for food. Some families include beans, rice, and eggs in their diet. The Rendille are not traders; only occasionally do they barter at markets for tea, sugar, or cloth.

Tea, milk, or sugar may be scarce in the dry season. At that time you can hear the older women chant a sad verse like this one:

Ngoko traya!	My grandchild!
majani makhabo	There are no tea leaves.
sulhal makhabo	There is no sugar.
oh! ngoko traya!	Oh! my grandchild!

Daily life often includes building new huts and getting water for the animals.

earrings. They finish the wooden milk containers used by men, and they also help make aluminum bracelets and clothing from goat hide. As a part of her dowry, each Rendille woman makes a mat called *ilal*. The *ilal* is woven from palm branches and secured with camel hide. It is then supported by bushes and covered with skins. It serves as a bed or couch for childbirth.

Livestock-rearing is different for the Ariaal. They raise camels but also cattle and smaller livestock. Also, the Ariaal have access to ample grazing land because of their strong ties with both the Northern Rendille and the Samburu.

The Northern Rendille use camels to pay fees and to slaughter at rituals, but the Ariaal use their camels only for food and transportation. They use cows for fees and rituals. Because they have ample camel milk, the Ariaal do not have to depend on cattle for food. Like the other Rendille, the Ariaal diet is mostly milk, with a little meat and corn. The Ariaal also bleed their animals to provide blood that is drunk by young male herders and women after childbirth.

▼ SETTLEMENTS ▼

The Rendille clans live in temporary settlements called *gobs* that are usually built near wells dug in the riverbeds. Generally a settlement is given the name of the clan, the subclan, or the elder of the family.

A typical settlement is made up of two dozen houses with about 120 inhabitants. The houses, made from acacia wood and wild sisal rope, can easily be carried when the settlement moves. Women are responsible for taking the houses apart and putting them back together in the new location. The Rendille shift settlements three to five times a year.

The Rendille make their own utensils, such as woven milk containers and spoons. They are

In the center of each settlement, the men build a ritual circle called *Nabo*. Here elders discuss problems and make decisions.

skilled craftsmen and make a wide variety of decorations and ornaments.

In the center of each settlement, the men build a ritual circle or enclosure called *Nabo* or *Naapo*. Here the elders meet to discuss problems and make decisions. As a rule, women are not allowed to enter the *Nabo*, and only elders may enter the central circle. The elders meet there for prayer and discussion of the day's events, to receive guests, and to perform ceremonies.

The Ariaal have separate settlements for camel-herding families and those who herd cattle. Those in the large camel settlements have close ties to the Northern Rendille. They speak the Rendille language and follow many of their rituals. In cattle settlements, the Samburu language is mostly spoken. In fact, those Ariaal think of themselves as Samburu. Each wife owns her own home, where she lives with her children.

▼ LIVESTOCK OR HERDING CAMPS ▼

The main herds are kept in camps called *forr*, which are built outside the family settlement. Each kind of livestock has its own camp. The Rendille have separate types of camps: sheep and goats, cattle, and camels.

The large herds of cattle and camels are cared for by unmarried herdsmen of the warrior age-set, fourteen to thirty years of age. Uncircumcised boys help with the herding. The most senior herdsmen are in charge of managing the herd. Unmarried girls, young boys, and some elders look after the small stock camps. The number of herders in a *forr* ranges from ten to sixty.▲

chapter

4

CUSTOMS AND RITUALS

RENDILLE CUSTOMS AND RITUALS RELATE TO
the age-set system, birth, marriage, death,
camel-herding, and clans. They are part of
everyday life.

▼ BIRTH ▼

Rendille women usually give birth at home,
helped by older women. Four days after a baby
boy is born, a male goat is sacrificed in celebration. The elders bless the child four times. For
four days the mother is allowed only to eat soup
and drink the blood of a male camel. She may
not drink milk for four months. Many rituals
involve the number four, which is sacred to
many peoples of East Africa. When a mother's
first child is a boy, she adopts a special hairstyle
called a *doko*. She wears her hair in the *doko*
until the death of her son or husband.

When a mother's first child is born, she adopts a special hairstyle called a *doko*.

The rituals are similar for the birth of a girl. A ewe goat is sacrificed instead of a ram. The child is blessed three times instead of four. The mother drinks blood for three days, not four. A ram is killed for the mother to eat after three days, and a goat is prepared for feasting by the whole settlement.

The Rendille believe that some babies bring bad luck. They are uneasy if a mother's first birth is twins. It is also considered bad luck if a boy is born on a Wednesday when there is no moon. Boys born on a moonless Wednesday are thought likely to become jealous of their older brothers and even to try to kill them.

▼ AGE-SET INITIATION ▼

Circumcision is the central act of initiation into an age-set. Each clan has its own special settlement and initiation hut for this ceremony. All of the young men who are eligible are circumcised in the same month. They receive gifts from older or richer men in the clan.

A young man sits on a stone to be circumcised. As long as he sits on the stone, he will keep receiving gifts. The other candidates must wait in line for him to decide that he has enough gifts. The elders of the settlement either encourage the youth's relatives to give more camels or encourage the youth to leave the stone.

After circumcision, the youths go to the initiation hut to recover. There they are instructed in how to behave as adults. Initiation carries important responsibilities to the community. During this period, the youths are not allowed to touch meat or anything made of iron, such as a knife or a spear.

In the year following circumcision, a major

The Rendille mark the culmination of many rituals by dancing.

ceremony called *Galgulumi* is held, at which an age-set is named. After an age-set has passed through *Galgulumi*, no other youths may join that age-set.

Galgulumi is held at a ceremonial site several miles wide. Huts are built in a huge fenced circle. At night, the two *moieties* separate from each other and bathe. A large circle is drawn in the center of the settlement, and elders place bowls of water and milk in it. The youths must drink from these bowls. Then there is singing and dancing by men of all age-grades. Women may only watch these ceremonies, which may last for several days.

The twelfth year after circumcision is thought

Married women wear necklaces and other ornaments made of hundreds of pearls, beads, and materials such as plant fibers.

to bring bad luck. A ceremony called *Orelogoraha* is held in that year is to keep evil away.

▼ MARRIAGE ▼

When a young man finds a woman he wants to marry, he gives her gifts of beads. If she accepts the beads, they are engaged. The man does not offer the gifts directly to the woman, however. Instead, a woman of the same age takes the beads to the bride's mother. For a while, a woman may not know what man is wooing her. She cannot accept beads from more than one man. Once she accepts beads from a man, she is expected to marry him.

Before marriage, a woman has her earlobes pierced and decorated with beads. She is also expected to have her body tattooed.

39

After the concluding ceremony of a wedding, a woman becomes a part of her husband's family.

Preparation for the wedding ceremony is lengthy. The prospective groom must give the bridewealth, or *gunu*, to the bride's family.

The bridewealth consists of four female and four male camels. The father of the bride receives two male and two female camels. The others are given to other members of the bride's family, and one is slaughtered and eaten at the wedding ceremony.

A married woman wears beautiful jewelry made of glass and metal. She wears necklaces of beads and wire, headbands, and large circular earrings. On top of the beads given by the husband, the bride's mother places an ornament called a *bukhurcha*, made from a special tree. Single women are allowed to wear only a necklace of white beads.

A woman joins her husband's family after marriage. She lives with his mother, stepmother, brothers, sisters, cousins, aunts, uncles, and even other men of his age-set.

▼ DEATH ▼

Certain ceremonial practices are associated with death. When a woman dies, she is carried with her eldest son holding her head and is buried near the entrance to her hut. She is placed in the grave on her left side. Both her husband and children shave their heads as a sign of mourning.

Before a man dies, his head should be shaved. If this cannot be done, a member of another clan is asked to shave instead. If he agrees, he is rewarded with stock from the dead man's herd. To shave your head for someone who has died is thought to be very risky, because it might bring you death.

The dead man is carried, with his eldest son holding his head, to a grave just opposite the entrance to his hut. The grave is only three feet long. He is laid on his right side, with arms and knees tucked up. Each person in the settlement places a stone and some earth on the body. The

Animal sacrifices are a part of many Rendille rituals and ceremonies.

man's shaved hair is scattered on top, and then the grave is covered with tree branches.

Two nights later, a pregnant ewe is killed, and parts of it are left by the grave. The dead man's hut is taken down to be cleansed, then set up again in another part of the settlement. Males closely related to the dead man are not allowed to eat red meat, drink blood, or engage in celebrations until the next moon.

Before the Rendille were subjected to British colonial government, they treated murderers harshly. A person who killed another by accident was not allowed to marry. No one would eat with him or cut his hair. A person who killed on purpose was stoned to death. When the British took control, murderers were fined and expected to pay large numbers of camels for their crime. The Rendille would not keep the rewards, however, considering them bad luck.

The Ariaal Rendille draw their customs, rituals, and culture both from the Northern Rendille and the Samburu. Like the Samburu, they believe that the world was created by Nkai, a supernatural force that causes the rain to fall and the grass to grow. They also share the Samburu belief in witches and ghosts. They sometimes ask advice of the Samburu *loibonok*, a person with supernatural power who can predict the future, protect against sorcery, and make medicines to bring fertility to a herd.

The Ariaal also believe in the *laisi*, the Rendille holy men. These men are less powerful than the *loibonok*, but their blessings and curses are still greatly respected. The Ariaal share certain Rendille rituals related to childbirth, burial of the dead, and camel-herding. For example, on a new moon, they light ritual fires beside their gateways. After an eclipse, they light fires on either side of the gates for the livestock to pass through. Every April they follow the *almhado*, the ritual blessing for the coming spring rains.

This sharing of customs and practices of the Rendille shows how open Ariaal society is to their neighbors. This flexibility exists in the economy as well. The fact that they have several

The Ariaal Rendille and the Samburu share many customs.

means of support—camels, cattle, and small livestock—has helped them survive times of crisis. At the same time, the mix has made it difficult to know their identity. The Northern Rendille think of the Ariaal as Rendille; they dress like Rendille and they are camel-herders. But the Ariaal are also cattle-herders and follow some Samburu customs.

The Ariaal are aware of this identity confusion. They call themselves "Samburu with camels," but on government lists they claim to be Rendille. However, they keep the name Ariaal to show that they are a unique people with a distinct society.▲

chapter

5

EUROPEAN CONTACT

DURING THE NINETEENTH CENTURY, MANY conflicts arose between the Rendille and their neighbors. The Bantu-speaking Ngoni raided from Tanzania in the south. The Turkana, moving south from the Sudan, overpowered the Rendille, Samburu, and Boran and took over part of their land. The Maasai were expanding from the plains of south central Kenya and challenged many of their neighbors for grazing land.

Besides these conflicts, the last decade of that century was known as "The Disaster." A series of disease epidemics, droughts, and famines killed off huge numbers of humans and animals. The camels of the Rendille survived the disease called rinderpest, but many of the Samburu cattle died. The Samburu were also seriously affected by the famine.

The Rendille were hit hardest by smallpox. By the end of the century, their population was

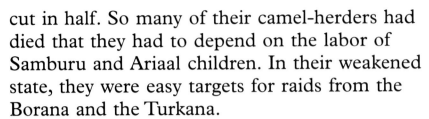

cut in half. So many of their camel-herders had died that they had to depend on the labor of Samburu and Ariaal children. In their weakened state, they were easy targets for raids from the Borana and the Turkana.

The Ariaal group was created around this time of Rendille who had fled the misfortunes of famine and disease. The Ariaal traded labor for Rendille livestock. In addition, they were able to use Samburu lands for grazing because of their close connection.

▼ BRITISH COLONIAL RULE ▼

Europeans first made regular contact with the Rendille in 1883. They brought a variety of items to trade for labor and also for ivory. The Rendille were interested in European brass, iron wire, Venetian beads, tobacco, and cloth.

In 1909 Great Britain began to set up a permanent colonial government. At a time when the Rendille were recovering from decades of bad fortune, the British began to take control of the region. They formed the Northern Frontier Province. By 1921 they had established a permanent administration over Rendille territory. The Rendille and Samburu were still so threatened by raids by the Borana and Turkana that they became allies of the British for their own protection.

To control the grazing lands for European

settlers, the British altered many traditions of the native peoples. In 1921, the Rendille and Samburu were confined to separate districts. They were separated further in 1934. The Rendille were moved to the Marsabit District in the Northern Frontier Province; the Samburu, to the Rift Valley Province.

In addition to controlling livestock, the British wanted to control the African societies. They tried to change a central feature of the Samburu social structure, the age-set system, and appointed chiefs to govern the Rendille according to British regulations. However, these attempts failed, and the Rendille remained the least controlled by the colonial government. As a result of British policies, however, some of the traditional ties between the Rendille and the Samburu were broken.

▼ AFTER INDEPENDENCE ▼

After a long struggle, Kenya gained its independence from Britain in 1963. The independent African government concerned itself with developing Rendille land, providing hospitals and schools, and teaching new methods of earning a living and running a business. These policies have had an important impact on the Rendille.▲

chapter

6

SOCIAL CHANGE

THE MAIN CAUSES OF CHANGE IN THE
Rendille societies have been the environment
and outside forces. Drought, famine, and disease
have been continuing problems. In addition,
contact with Europeans, the British colonial
government, and finally Kenyan independence
have all brought major changes in traditional
ways of life.

The drought and disease at the end of the
nineteenth century were the main reason for
the formation of Ariaal society, as we have seen.
The Ariaal created a way of life that was flexible
and open to their neighbors so that they could
survive nearly anything. However, this was a
major change for the Rendille people as a whole.
Before the Ariaal, the Rendille depended only
on each other, but now they had to admit how
much they needed the help of their neighbors.

During British colonial rule, the Rendille, and many other peoples of eastern Africa, began to move into the cities and accept Western education.

▼ THE MARKET ECONOMY ▼

When the Europeans began to come to
East Africa in the late nineteenth century, the
African peoples slowly became Westernized.
Because the Rendille were nomads, they were
not so directly influenced by the newcomers.
At first the Rendille were not much interested
in the maize, tobacco, beads, cloth, and
ostrich feathers brought by the Europeans
and the Swahili and Somali traders from the
coast.

The long period of British colonial rule
eventually brought changes in culture and
economy for the Rendille, however. In time,
they became part of the market economy. They
left behind traditional ways of survival and
began to exchange labor and goods for services and money from the outside world. They
began to move into the cities and accept
Western education.

At first, the British encouraged only small
trading posts in Rendille country. Indian and
Somali traders sold tea, sugar, cloth, and canned
goods. In 1935, however, the British demanded
that the people of the region pay taxes. The
Rendille had no choice but to sell either their
livestock or their own labor for cash.

During the 1930s, the British demanded that
the pastoralists sell much of their cattle at low
prices. They feared African competition with

Despite the defeat of the Mau Mau movement, Kenya won
independence in 1963.

their own beef industry. The British also seized
the richest farming land and gave it to European
settlers, forcing the original inhabitants to live in
overcrowded reserves.

By the late 1940s, the African peoples had
had enough of British control. They rebelled in
the Mau Mau revolution, a violent movement
of liberation. Mau Mau was finally stopped
by violent arrests. Despite the defeat of Mau
Mau, Kenyan independence was won in 1963.

▼ MODERNIZATION ▼

Like the British, the new African government wanted the people to sell their livestock. Their purpose, however, was to modernize Kenya.

The government policy has worked. The Rendille now buy much more maize, sugar, tea, tobacco, clothes, and shoes. Many Rendille women wear modern clothes, although most still prefer the traditional animal skins, which are thought better adapted to a pastoral life.

The Rendille still experience drought and famine. In 1971–73 and again in 1982–84, both the Rendille and the Ariaal lost much of their livestock. The Rendille dealt with these crises by settling permanently around Catholic mission relief stations. The Ariaal survived the disasters and continued their nomadic life-style.

The Kenyan government has asked organizations such as the United Nations and religious missions for help in the development of the country. These agencies dig wells and build roads. They provide food during times of famine. There is some fear that the peoples will become too dependent on help from outside. The mission at Korr was recently made into a permanent town of 5,000 Rendille.

However, efforts are being made to teach practices that will allow the peoples to live more independently in a modernized country. The United Nations Educational, Scientific, and

Cultural Organization (UNESCO) and other groups are trying to develop and teach methods of cattle-herding that will use the land more effectively and increase production.

The Rendille have settled around centers of access to water, schools, and shops, but new problems crop up. Permanent settlements lead to overgrazing, so that more grasslands are turning into deserts.

The government has tried to improve health care, veterinary care, education, roads, communication, electricity, and local administration. But the more these modernizing policies are instituted, the more the African peoples leave behind their traditional ways of life. It may be that the Northern Rendille have changed their life-style too much to return to their traditional systems. But the Ariaal, because of their greater flexibility, have been able to keep more of their traditional herding way of life.

When asked about their life and customs, the Rendille are open with their opinions. The Rendille have taken up cattle and small stock, but they still clearly prefer camels. Small stock and cattle are used for food, to sell for cash, clothes, and other goods, and for traditional social purposes. Camels are still the livestock used to pay a brideprice. They also represent security to the Rendille, because camels are successful in difficult climates.

Few Rendille are happy with the many changes occurring within their culture.

The Rendille have mostly negative feelings about settling down permanently. Staying in the same place all the time has changed their culture and customs. For example, women have had to change the feeding of their children. Because milk is in short supply, they have to go to the market and buy expensive substitutes.

Permanent settlements are also thought to encourage people to have children, which leads to overpopulation. At the same time, many Rendille children now go to school, so the young men are not available for herding. This makes it impossible to take the livestock to distant grazing lands. But if the animals always graze in the same area, that land turns to desert. To help solve this problem, households cooperate and take turns herding each other's animals.

The decline of the Rendille nomadic life is changing the social system. The elders no longer receive the respect they once did. They no longer have control over the youth. As education becomes more available, it is easier to find work outside the Rendille community. When youths need not depend on herding to make a living, they become less dependent on their parents.

The Rendille are divided in their opinions about these changes. Almost half of them think that schools, famine relief, medical care, and Christianity are good new things. However, many Rendille are not happy about the changes.

▼ SPIRITUAL BELIEFS ▼

The Rendille have combined some ideas from Christianity with traditional beliefs. To them God is the source of all life. They think of God

The Rendille have combined some ideas from Christianity with traditional beliefs.

as alive, because only living things can give life. He is invisible, all-powerful, and all-knowing. But just as God gives life, he also takes it away through death and disease. For the Rendille, the living things in the universe include the clouds. Rain falls from the clouds, and rain is a source of life. The air we breathe is also a source of life.

Rendille ancestors are believed to live underground as spirits and to have power over their descendants. If they are angry they can cause disease among the living. It is therefore important to follow rituals carefully to show respect to the ancestors. A person who dies becomes an ancestral spirit, but is always very much involved with the living.

▼ **THE ELDERS AND THE FUTURE** ▼

The Rendille elders are faced with making big decisions for their community. These decisions are guided by their image of the future.

The elders generally are unhappy with the changes in their society. The hardships of recurring periods of drought call for decisions that affect their own survival. They see the present age-set as weak because they are so dependent on help in crises and have given up much of their traditional way of life.

In the last few decades, the Rendille have again decided to rely on outsiders to help them through droughts and famine, the same decision made a hundred years ago after the famine and the smallpox epidemic. However, it has the unwanted effect of making the Rendille dependent on long-term aid. They have become used to food and goods that they cannot produce themselves. This creates a need for cash, but there is not enough employment for everyone.

The activities of relief agencies also bring about cultural change. A major change is that many young people are converting to Catholicism. This angers the Rendille elders, who have even threatened to forbid marriages with converts.

The elders also are worried about Western education. It draws today's young Rendille away from the clan system and makes them less

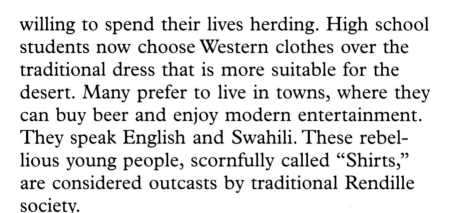

willing to spend their lives herding. High school students now choose Western clothes over the traditional dress that is more suitable for the desert. Many prefer to live in towns, where they can buy beer and enjoy modern entertainment. They speak English and Swahili. These rebellious young people, scornfully called "Shirts," are considered outcasts by traditional Rendille society.

Clan loyalty may still be important to the youth, but because of their education they see the world very differently. They have new perspectives on herding practices, the cause and cure of diseases, and the importance of individual freedom. By converting to Catholicism, Protestantism, and Islam, they are exercising individual spiritual freedom but moving away from their traditions. They are separating themselves from traditional Rendille society. Many of them are unemployed, while others find jobs with the local government services.

Today the Rendille face a sharp clash between traditional values and the Westernization of their youth. They face a crisis in the economic system. These two major changes together could mean the end of the clan system as well as the age-set system. The Rendille are becoming dependent on food and aid from outside.

Most Rendille believe that their society can be improved by more modern ways of livestock-herding. They are also glad to have schools, roads, and hospitals to help their children survive in today's world. But they would like such important changes to be made with the input of the elders and the support of the Rendille people. In this way, perhaps, progress can be made without losing touch with what it means to be Rendille.▲

Glossary

age-grades Periods of life that every Rendille passes through.

age-set All of the males from a fourteen-year period who are ready to leave boyhood and become youths.

bridewealth Camels paid by a man to his bride's family.

clan Group of families who trace their roots back to the same ancestor.

Cushitic One of the three language groups of Kenya. Rendille is a Cushitic language.

Dablakabire Youth chosen to take the blame for all the misfortunes that touch his age-set.

Disaster, the Name given to the last ten years of the ninteenth century, a period of drought, famine, and disease.

doko Special hairstyle worn by a woman if her first child is a boy.

Galgulumi (*Galgurme*) Ceremony held a year after circumcision.

laisi Rendille holy men with the power to bless and curse.

loibonok Samburu diviner and medicine man who advises the Ariaal.

Mau Mau Violent movement in Kenya in the late 1940s that helped to bring Kenyan independence from Britain.

moieties Two halves of a society, from which clans are formed.

Nabo (*Naapo*) Ceremony to show that youths are ready to become married elders.

Nkai Supernatural power that the Rendille believe brings life to the world.

Odola Rendille Group of Rendille who live near the Gabbra people.

Orelogoraha Ceremony held in the twelfth year after circumcision, to ward off evil.

totem Object or animal that is a sacred symbol of a particular clan.

True Rendille Another name for the Northern Rendille.

Tumal The class of blacksmiths, who do not belong to any clan.

For Further Reading

Breeden, R. L. *Nomads of the World*. Washington, DC: National Geographic Society, 1971.

Clark, Leon. E. *Through African Eyes: The Past Road to Independence*, rev. ed. New York: Center for International Training and Education, 1991.

Fedders, Andre, and Salvatori, Cynthia. *Peoples and Cultures of Kenya*. Nairobi: TransAfrica, 1979.

Garlake, Peter. *The Kingdoms of Africa*, rev. ed. New York: Peter Berick Books, 1990.

Jones, David K. *Shepherd of the Desert*. London: Elm Tree Books, 1984.

Challenging Reading

Lamb, David. *The Africans*. New York: Random House, 1987.

Moss, Joyce, and Wilson, George. *People of the World: Africans South of the Sahara*. Detroit: Gale Research Inc., 1991.

Were, Gideon, and Wilson, D. A. *East Africa Through a Thousand Years*, rev. ed. London: Evans Brothers, 1972.

Index

ACKNOWLEDGMENTS

I should like to express my thanks to Marie Monteagudo, reference librarian at William Paterson College, for her help in gaining access to the rare documents, photographs, and films used for this research. I should also like to thank Joanne M. Zellers of the African and Middle Eastern Division of the Library of Congress and all the staff of the Schomburg Center for Research in Black Culture for their generous assistance.

ABOUT THE AUTHOR

Dr. Ronald G. Parris is Chairman of the Department of African, African-American, and Caribbean Studies at William Paterson College. He is also founding Director of the Ralph Bunche Institute of International Studies. Previously he served at the United Nations Educational, Scientific, and Cultural Organization (UNESCO), Paris, where he was responsible for programs on rural development, international migration, population, and the environment. In that capacity, he traveled widely in Africa, Europe, and the Americas.

Dr. Parris grew up in Barbados, West Indies, before coming to the United States for his college education. He holds a PhD in Sociology from Yale University. He lives in Montclair, New Jersey.

PHOTO CREDITS

AP/Wide World Photo (pp. 49, 51); CFM, Nairobi (all other photos)

PHOTO RESEARCH

Vera Ahmadzadeh with Jennifer Croft

DESIGN

Kim Sonsky